Praise for Flying for Beginners

"It's official! We all hear voices! *Flying for Beginners* reveals the inner workings and powerful influence of our internal dialogue. Taking us on an intimate journey we encounter different aspects of ourselves to discover our true friend and voice of wisdom. This is a book for those who want to build lasting confidence from the inside out. Full of genuine story, compassion for self, practical insight, tips and strategies to rescript your life. Beware, this read may change your life!"

— Sue Liburd MBE, Human Capital Entrepreneur

"*Flying For Beginners* takes the reader on a triumphant journey of self-discovery and inner cohesion. Easily assimilated and effective in its approach, Jo Emerson's book unlocks our limited thinking and opens the door to a new world of limitless outcome."

— Susan Winter, relationship expert and best-selling author of *Allowing Magnificence*

Flying for Beginners

A Proven System for Lasting Self-Confidence

By Jo Emerson

Flying for Beginners:
A Proven System for Lasting Self-Confidence
By Jo Emerson

www.jo-emerson.com
Published by Jo Emerson

Acknowledgements

I'm one of the luckiest people on earth as I'm surrounded by a team of amazing friends (aka cheerleaders) who've believed in me as a coach from the word go. So, Pete, Andrew, Norma, Erica, William and Dulcie — thank you so much. This book would still be languishing in a word document were it not for the incredible creative skills of Becca Astrop. Thanks to you, Becca, I have a published book, which is a dream come true. I am forever indebted to the very special people in my life with whom I can honestly share my truth. Much of what you find in this book echoes what I've learnt during those life-affirming conversations. I am also indebted to Sarah, Pam and Delma from whom I started learning to be myself and to manage my thoughts, and to my three besties, Rach, Zoe and Livs, who have loved me through thick and thin for over 30 years. Finally, deep thanks must go to my courageous clients (especially Tom, Jude and Danny, whose names have been changed) who have allowed me so generously into the nooks and crannies of their lives. Seeing their growth and change is unbelievably rewarding and one of life's greatest privileges.

This book is dedicated to my three gorgeous daughters — Beth, Eva and Nancy — who have taught me the meaning of love and family.

Flying for Beginners

A Proven System for Lasting Self-Confidence

People used to tell me to 'believe in myself' and 'love myself' and I used to think, *I would if you could tell me how!* But, no one could. So, with characteristic dogged determination (and a belief that surely life had to be better and happier than it had been for me thus far), I set about finding out how one learns to love and believe in oneself, how one gains lasting confidence and true self-esteem. And here it is. This work has changed my life, I truly wish the same for you.

Contents

In a Nutshell

This is a little book about a big problem. Huge numbers of us lack confidence and self-belief and most of us don't know why. We think it's due to what happened to us as children or the circumstances of our lives today. (I'm not for a minute suggesting these things don't have an effect on us, but I do know we can choose now whether to be rooted in them or not.)

But that is not really why we lack confidence. We lack self-esteem and confidence because we *believe* the negative chatter in our heads and we *act* upon it, which makes us feel even lower. It's a vicious cycle; one I was caught up in for years. Today, however, I know how to escape the vicious cycle and I have the daily privilege of helping my clients do the same.

In this book, I will show you what the root of your problem is and, crucially, how to overcome it. This is not a quick fix — these are new habits you will need to learn and practise in order to be free. But, when you are free you will experience life in a totally new way; one in which you are happy to be yourself, contributing your best to the world unplagued by the fear, doubt and worry you've been dragging around with you thus far.

This book will help you if you are crippled by low self-esteem, or if you simply have annoying moments of self-doubt — who doesn't? It will help you understand the link between what you are thinking and feeling and how these manifest to create the reality of your life.

While I was buying my coffee this morning I was telling the barista that I was writing a book about managing the chatter in our heads and he said, "Oh yes, we all have that negative voice — the trick is not to let other people see it!"

But for me it goes deeper than that. It's not about hiding it away from others. It's about facing it, finding out what it's up to and then gaining the power to let what it says go if you choose to. This book is about giving you the ultimate choice: which of your thoughts to believe and which to discard. Using my system will enable you to drop the masks behind which you hide and to live with authenticity and freedom.

If you are ready to make some powerful changes in your life this book is for you. If you are ready to give up some old patterns of thought and behaviour then this book is for you. If you are desperate to overcome anxiety and reach your potential this book is absolutely for you.

Please be encouraged that change is very, very possible. I've changed dramatically, as have my clients (some of whom you'll meet in this book) and if we can do it, so can you. This book isn't long because it doesn't need to be. It's designed to be read cover to cover fairly quickly and then used as a manual as you grow and change. Use it to pinpoint what you need to work on, take heart from the stories, do the exercises and then relax while your subconscious reshuffles and your life begins to improve.

What's Going On?

Chapter 1

My Story

Until recent years, fear underpinned my life and I felt I'd been seeking peace and happiness forever but never quite finding what I was looking for. I was a self-help book junkie whose life never changed for more than a few days or weeks. I was forever starting a new regime only to fail and then beat myself up for that failure.

I was looking for the answers outside myself (in weight-loss, approval from people, relationships, food, drink, excessive exercise, religious thinking, etc.) and yet nothing seemed to be fixing me. I was often unhappy, self-loathing and ashamed, and I was deeply disconnected from myself — not that you would've guessed: I was outwardly very confident and gregarious. I had a good life, lovely children, great job, etc., but I was constantly questioning myself, holding myself up to comparison against others, trying to fix how I felt about things that had happened in the past and worrying about what might happen in the future. It was relentless and exhausting.

As a child, I was very afraid of life but learnt to mask my feelings of low self-esteem by being studious, gregarious and determined. I was a people pleaser and gained huge amounts of self-esteem and self-belief when I felt others approved of me. Of course, this feeling never lasted so I continually sought more and more approval.

These feelings of low self-esteem continued into my teens and twenties despite graduating with a great degree, travelling the world and building a fairly successful career. I was unhappy at my core (although, of course, there were many happy moments) and felt thoroughly inadequate. I could no sooner spend time undistracted from my own anxious thoughts and feelings than I could build a rocket ship. Peace was an anathema to me. To the outside world I probably appeared to be an ambitious, go-getting, fun-loving twenty-something but deep down all I wanted was for someone to please tell me how to 'do life'. My constant companion (except when inebriated or lost in work or exercise) was this underlying sense of fear and doom approaching. And I questioned myself all the time! I mean, ALL the time.

I was quite good at my job but there was always that chirruping voice in my head:

They're going to find out about you! You're no good at this really! Who do you think you are doing this?

I was a normal sized woman but that voice would tell me:

You're not good enough as a size 12. Women should be skinny and little and men should be able to pick them up easily. You should be a size 8, you should be thinner, you shouldn't be eating, you should be better at dieting.

This voice went on and on and on and I believed it, so I continued to try to change the way I looked. I just kept trying to be thin in order to be approved of. By whom? By myself. I was unacceptable to myself.

I sought answers wherever I went and yet could not seem to find them. Even adopting religion for a while did nothing to quell my fear (in fact, it probably made it worse). The chirruping voice continued to tell me that I wasn't good enough at work, as a woman, as a mother, etc., and that it was likely that something terrible was going to happen. In short, the voice of fear got louder and louder, and the louder it got, the more I believed it.

I think it's worth noting at this point that I am, of course, talking about this time of my life with the benefit of hindsight because when I was living it, I wasn't aware that there was a particular 'voice' in my head. It had always been there so, rather like the sky, I didn't question its existence or usefulness — it was just 'there'.

I do know that I absolutely believed everything it said.

I considered it to be the voice of truth and I honestly believed that if I didn't do what it said then something terrible might happen. My low self-esteem wouldn't have even entertained the thought that I could question that voice. I guess I kind of knew that there was a harshness to it, but who was I to question its authority? The voice was right: I was rubbish at life and the best thing I could do would be to continue trying to hide that fact from others.

And so that voice ruled the roost, keeping me in my place until…

…My life changed dramatically several years ago. I lost a friend to suicide, had a serious health scare myself, and left my marriage. In the shock of it all, and despite the grief and anguish, I had clarity for what felt like the first time, so I began to search inside myself for the answers that I'd been seeking elsewhere.

I'd run out of options 'out there' but to even start the process of looking inward was a frightening concept to me — after all, who was I to decide what was right or wrong for my life? Surely someone else knew better?

I see now that my self-esteem was on the floor. I was also highly reluctant to take responsibility for my life — I had always thought it was safer to follow someone else's rules, all the while getting more and more frustrated with the restrictions I was accepting and my inability to live up to them. I sought help from various people and started becoming aware of the different parts of my personality. Through research, I was able to identify that there was a very critical voice in my head that I was very afraid of and that I treated like a parent who had to be obeyed. However, I was also aware of another, more childlike energy within myself and a wiser, kinder voice buried deep, deep within.

Knowing I'd stumbled on something profound, I started to get to know these different parts of me by allowing and encouraging them to speak in my (at that stage, sporadic) journaling. I started to understand what the different parts of me wanted, what their motivations were, and I noticed an interesting pattern. When I believed that angry, scared voice in my head (that critical voice) I felt deep anxiety and fear, but when I challenged it with kindness and wisdom the fear and the anxiety lessened or left.

My situation hadn't changed but my response to it had. I played around with this for several weeks (becoming more dedicated in my journaling for a time) just noting what was going on inside me, pondering, watching, waiting, observing and being curious. Part of me wanted to leap in and start fixing my thoughts but I knew at that time my job was just to observe what was going on. It was one of the greatest times of healing in my life, as I finally became reunited with myself, accepting of myself and believing in who I was. I dedicated time to listening to myself rather than doing whatever I could to avoid facing myself.

But there was still more, and the day came when I realised that I had a choice as to whether I believed that critical voice or not. And what followed went something like this:

I made a decision to take 24 hours off from believing the critical voice. I'm aware this sounds crazy and perhaps it is, but it worked. I realised that this voice was a part of me and that I couldn't get rid of it completely.

I was still afraid of not doing what it said, and yet I knew that I needed to give myself a chance, so I negotiated with myself. I said to this voice:

I'm going to take 24 hours off from believing you; you who is an internalised version of a critical, angry, controlling parent, godhead, schoolyard bully. I'm going to experiment with a day of not believing what you say. Waffle on if you must but I won't be engaging in conversation with you today.

Then, with all the courage I could muster I stood at the metaphorical cliff edge (that's honestly how it felt — quite terrifying) and I prepared to jump. I was both petrified and exhilarated at the prospect. I didn't know what I was going to find on the other side, but I knew I was going to jump because I knew I had to unhook from that voice if I was going to survive the rest of my life without developing a serious neurosis.

So I did jump, and in that moment of unhooking and metaphorical leaping I realised I had wings! I could fly! I realised I'd been believing a lie for years. I realised I was free. I was free to make mistakes and that it would be OK. I was free to explore life and make my own decisions. I was free to believe nice things about myself. I was free to love. I was free to play. I was free to be afraid sometimes and not let it crush me. I was free of the overwhelming opinions of others. I was free to be an authentic version of myself and I was free from having to believe the controlling, shaming fear from that voice.

And did I go back as I had promised? No, but that voice is still a part of me and I've learnt to compassionately manage it. That voice still chirrups away but I have a choice over whether or not I believe it today. When I exercise that choice, I have so much more inner peace.

When I believed the critical voice my life was very, very black and white. Good or bad. Perfection or failure. Now, life is a good old balanced mixture of everything. Now I have a choice, life is a range of colours, a range of emotions that are sometimes strong, sometimes gentle and often in between. The wise voice I've found inside never leaves me and has never let me down. The more I choose to listen to it the more fear leaves my life and, most importantly, the same is true for the clients with whom I share this work.

This book is called *Flying for Beginners* because when you

make your own metaphorical cliff-edge leap, you'll discover you have wings and can fly too. This book is called *Flying for Beginners* because I know from my own experience that when I unhooked from that voice I genuinely felt I was flying and I'd love to teach you how to fly too.

A caveat

Some of the concepts used in this book may make you uncomfortable — ideas like Inner Child and Inner Voices can make even the most impassioned analyst want to reach for the bucket. I get that! However, if you can suspend your awkwardness for the time it takes to do the exercises in this book, I know you'll be glad you did.

I've done my best to neutralise the squirm factor but we are still going to be talking about voices in your head and parts of your personality. Why? Because these concepts really do nail it in terms of what's going on in your mind, so please bear with me. You'll come to terms with it eventually and learn a whole heap about why you do what you do in the process.

Just to warn you there's a potentially awkward bit at the beginning of Chapter 7, so if you'd rather get it all over with in one hit please nip ahead to that section now before coming back to me here when you're done.

Chapter 2

Manage Your Mind

In my work as a coach I see people every day on my courses and face-to-face who struggle with a lack of self-belief, low self-esteem and either a complete lack of confidence or a shortage of confidence in one specific area of their life. And, it's my job (and my joy!) to help them change that.

Without question, every client I see (from company directors and entrepreneurs to senior managers, small business owners, teenagers, full-time parents and everyone else in between,) who suffers with low confidence to one extent or another, has become rooted in or hooked by the negative voice in their heads. They believe what it says and usually have done for years. It may not have ruled the roost entirely but in the areas it's been allowed to reign it has caused great fear and stress.

So, my first job is to help my client identify this voice and disassociate from it in order for them to see what's going on in their own mind. The first reaction I often see in my client is relief that they are not the only one to have 'voices' (we all do!) followed swiftly by a sense of regret and frustration that they have listened to it for so long. Others have always known it's been there but have resigned themselves to its presence and power in their lives.

For some people the chatter is incessant, for others it comes and goes. For some the chatter is loud and demanding, for others it's sneakier and subtler in its undermining. In all cases it's my job to encourage my client to hear and name that voice and then to help them see that they have a choice over whether to believe what it says or not. From here most people then want to find a way forward, a way out of the fog, a way to understand themselves better and to make choices to do things differently in future. In this case, knowledge really is power. Knowing what your mind is up to gives you the power to choose what to do with it.

The good news is that you don't need a face-to-face session with me to do this work because I can teach you how to better manage your thoughts yourself. That's what this book is about: understanding your thought processes so that you can make clearer, more confident choices about what you believe and how you live your life. This book comprises a thought-management system that I've developed through research, personal experience and that of my clients. And it works!

Unmanaged voices in your head can either boost your confidence or destroy your confidence. Think about how you might speak to a child. If you use words of encouragement to uplift that child, words to boost them and make them believe they can achieve what they want to achieve, then the chances are that child is going to act on your words and feel positively about themselves and the situation they are in.

However, if you speak negatively to a child and tell them that the world is scary, and that they probably shouldn't try that thing because they might fail, and that failure is a terrible thing, and that people will laugh at them if they make a mistake… then you are going to raise a child who is afraid and lacking in confidence.

Now imagine that child lives within you. Ask yourself how you speak to that child that is you. For a lot of us this is an 'ouch' moment, as we realise we're not very nice to ourselves. That's OK — acknowledging this will enable you to change.

Most of us are our own worst critics, which means that we are living with a constant stream of negative, fearful, critical thoughts that we can't escape because they're in our own heads. We are crushing ourselves! But the great news is that when we can identify that critical voice and understand its motivations we can take a decision to unhook from it and believe something else.

When we've been given the tools to deal with this critical voice, to build a relationship with the kinder and wiser part of ourselves and listen to it, we become happier and more fulfilled. Our confidence rises, our self-esteem is boosted and we start to believe in ourselves and our abilities to achieve and overcome things in life.

I believe everyone deserves a chance to live free from the tyranny of that critical voice. You deserve a chance to think freely and live freely in order to happily be who you really are. At the very least you deserve a choice! And, I truly believe, because I've done it myself and I help my clients to do it, that it is totally possible to see yourself and the world completely differently, if you believe something different in the first place.

On this journey I'll teach you how to identify what's going on inside you and give you exercises to get to know yourself a bit better. You may feel a massive sense of reluctance to do this but please do your best to plough on. Many people think they can't 'go there' (into their own minds) because it's too painful or too scary. In my opinion this is double-crossing courtesy of that critical, fearful voice. It doesn't want to be exposed for fear it will be banished. So, reassure it that it won't and can't be banished, that you simply want to learn what it needs in order to be saner and happier.

It's also worth me reassuring you that in my experience, the fear of facing something is always worse than the pain of actually facing it. Our fear keeps us locked and imprisoned in old patterns of thought and behaviour but freedom is always waiting on the other side if we can muster the courage to face our demons.

I've lost count of the number of clients I've seen who think this work is a 'good idea' but initially procrastinate about doing it because it's 'too scary' to go there. However, once the pain and frustration in their lives reaches a fever pitch they cave in, do this work and wonder why they didn't do it sooner. This is freedom on a plate, people, so muster all the courage, openness and honesty you can find and dive in!

You are worth this small investment of time to uncover the truth of what's going on in your mind in order for you to be able to do something differently in future.

Oh, and please remember that there is no such thing as perfection so aim for progress as you learn this new way of thinking and behaving.

So, are you ready to delve inside your mind to see what's going on?

Chapter 3

The Cast List

You are not your thoughts. I repeat — you are not your thoughts. Your life may be (in part) the product of your thoughts, but you are not them.

You, the essence of you, are the *observer*, the *curator* and the *manager* of your thoughts, or at least this is what you can become (and it's what the happiest, calmest people I know do).

For many years I was lost in my thoughts and they were my masters. I've now learnt to master them (most of the time) and so can you. In fact, these days I occasionally experience those blissful moments of 'no thought', which is miraculous considering the incessant chatter I lived with for decades. But the first step is to detach from the belief that you are your thoughts, because you are not.

If you're like me you'll find that an alien concept to begin with, but if you spend some time chewing this over you'll see that just as you are not your blood vessels, your fingernails or your sense of smell, you are also not your thoughts. These things are a part of you, but they are not you. You are the conscious awareness of these things.

This idea is vital if you are lacking in self-esteem or have anxiety or confidence issues, because often people with these problems are both terrorised by and identified by their critical thoughts. They believe what the fearful, negative voice has to say.

However, you can learn to disentangle yourself from your thoughts, listen to them and then to decide which are truthful and which are fanciful. Your thoughts can be rooted in fear, control and self-centredness; or love, truth and acceptance.

In short, believing the fearful voice and being defined by it is the cause of your unhappiness, anxiety and fear. It's the cause of your procrastination and dissatisfaction with yourself and the world around you.

You can choose to obey either voice (the fearful, controlling one or the loving, accepting one), but by listening to and heeding the words of the second voice on a more regular basis, you will grow in confidence and have a happier, more productive and peaceful life.

So, why don't we all do this? Because we've never been taught how to, and we've believed the lie that the fearful thoughts are the truth. I'm here to tell you that they're not and that you don't have to do what they say any more.

Really? Yes, really!

I am indebted to the work of Freud, Berne and others for their teachings about the different parts of our brains (or personalities), which provided me with the key to unlocking my own life and subsequently the lives of my clients. Understanding what goes on in your mind will give you the power to choose which thoughts you run with and which to merely listen to, but not necessarily act on. This work will change your life — are you ready?

Imagine…

Imagine you've been stuck in a job you hate for years but have lacked the confidence to leave. Maybe the voice in your head has been telling you:

You should be grateful to have a job. You'd lose all your financial security if you left. And what else would you do anyway?

Those thoughts would have no doubt contributed to you staying in the job you hated.

Now, imagine you hear about a job that would be perfect for you. The right hours, and a great position in a company you admire. You get excited as you think about applying and what it might feel like to get that job when the voice of doubt pipes up again:

You probably wouldn't get it. There are bound to be loads of far better qualified people than you applying for it. And, what if you forget what to say in the interview?

How do you feel? Despondent and demoralised, and highly unlikely to go for the thing you really want.

Now, imagine what would happen if your wisest friend could open up your mind and see the thoughts you were saying to yourself and believing. Imagine they could inject a few of their own thoughts into the mix to give you an alternative viewpoint, something like:

You'd be a real asset to that company! How exciting! What have you got to lose in applying? I know you're scared but even if you don't get it at least you will have tried. Staying where you are will only leave you feeling more frustrated. I believe in you — go for it!

Notice that when you listen to your friend's voice you feel more empowered, more able and more likely to at least have a go.

At this stage many of us worry, *But which is the voice of truth?* And the answer is, they both could be and it's up to you to prove either right. You can believe the negativity and this will become your reality or you can believe the positivity, give it a go and learn what you need to learn from the process. One voice keeps you safe and small and stuck, the other leads you to growth, exploration and opportunity. Crucially, one voice steals your energy and the other fills you up with positivity.

Oh, and guess what? That friend who peered into your brain is actually already inside you — it's you at your best, your wisest and your kindest — so no open-brain surgery required. I'll help you find your best, wisest, kindest self in the next chapter.

The three players

As we've established, we all have different voices in our heads. In fact, most of us have many, many different voices (or parts to our personalities, if you prefer). Just knowing that might make you feel a little better about yourself — you're not mad, it's perfectly normal to have different types of mental chatter buzzing away in your brain. What's wrong is that many of us have not been taught how to manage it. Until now…

So what's going on?

One way to view our 'voices' is to imagine:

- a Parent or critical voice
- a childlike voice (or Feeling Centre)
- and a wiser, more Adult voice

Try not to get too hung up on the nouns I've used, you'll choose your own in a bit and we'll look at them in more detail in the next chapter. So, what do I mean by 'voices'?

I'd like you to locate the part of yourself that gives you a hard time. It might say something like the following:

You should be thinner! You'll never make it! What are they saying about you? Why are you even trying? You can't do it perfectly so don't bother…! You're not as good as him… She's prettier than you. You should've known better! People can't be trusted.

Just sit for a moment, take a few deep breaths and locate that voice. Where does it live about your person? For a lot of us it's in the head area although some people find this voice in their chest, on their shoulder, behind their heads, etc. Find yours now — it doesn't matter where it lives, you just need to know where it is so you can locate it and identify when it's speaking to you.

Found it? Good. Make a mark on the body diagram (or draw your own) to show where this voice lives within you. This part of the process is crucial to your success so please don't skip this!

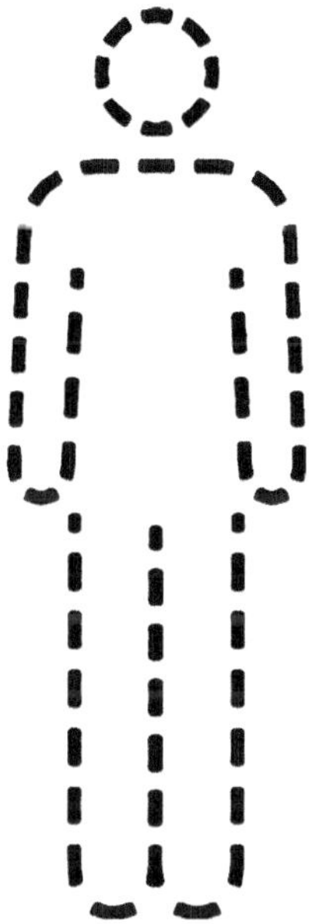

Now, I'd like you to notice what happens to your body when you listen to this voice. What do you feel when you are told you are a joke, that you should be thinner/ smarter/ richer/ younger, etc.? Anxious? Afraid? Angry? High energy or low? Whatever you feel, I'd like you to locate **where** you feel it. A lot of us feel these things in our high stomachs or lower chests but you might be different and that's fine. The point of this exercise is to locate where you feel your feelings and then make another mark on the diagram.

So, by now you should have two marks on the diagram. Lastly, I'd like you to locate the voice of reason and kindness you have either within you or close by to you. This is the voice you might use if you were helping a friend in crisis or it might be the imaginary voice of a wise friend. You will recognise this voice as it's more detached than the others and comes with a sense of balance. You may have to dig really deep to find it or you may have to imagine the voice of another person (a coach, a friend, an old, wise teacher or colleague). Now, notice where this voice is. For some of us this is right at our core, others sense this voice just to the side of themselves, in yet others it's further inside their minds. Again, at this stage I just need you to locate this voice and mark it on the diagram.

Well done. Please label your first mark as Critic or Parent, the second as Feelings or Child and the third as Wisdom or Adult.

When I first stumbled across this work I realised I had a fearful, controlling Gremlin located around on the right side of my head and shoulder. I also had a spirited, freedom-seeking Angel Fish(!) in my tummy and a Wise Friend standing just beside me (this has since moved to being a voice I experience both inside and outside of me.)

The names and locations of these 'parts' have been vital in my understanding of what's going on at any given time and where I might be off-kilter. These places (head: Gremlin, tummy: Angel Fish and to my side: Wise Friend) are where I go mentally and where I often gesture to or touch now when I want to discover what's happening in my inner world and figure out what I need to do to take care of myself.

Interestingly, I no longer use the names 'Gremlin' or 'Angel Fish' as they've been replaced with 'Critic' and 'Feelings' but being able to characterise these parts to begin with was crucial. Oh, and 'Wise Friend' has evolved to become 'Wisdom'.

So, let's learn more about yours. Find a comfortable, quiet place and take five deep breaths. When you feel relaxed and centred, turn the page and answer the following questions to ascertain the unique personalities of your different voices. Please take your time with this but don't overthink it! Your gut feeling will guide you to the truth in this work.

Your Parent/ Critical Voice

- Where does this voice live about your body?
- Is this voice male, female or without gender?
- If this voice had a colour, what would it be?
- What tone does this voice use when speaking to you?
- If this voice was an animal what would it be?
- Who does this voice most remind you of?
- What would be a suitable name for you to use when referring to this voice?

Your Child/ Feeling Part

- Where does this part live about your body?
- Is this part male, female or without gender?
- If this part had a colour, what would it be?
- What tone of voice does this part use when speaking to you?
- If this part was an animal what would it be?
- Who does this part most remind you of?
- What would be a suitable name for you to use when referring to this part?

Your Adult/ Wise Voice

- Where does this voice live, whether inside or outside your body?
- Is this voice male, female or without gender?
- If this voice had a colour, what would it be?
- What tone does this voice use when speaking to you?
- If this voice was an animal what would it be?
- Who does this voice most remind you of?
- What would be a suitable name for you to use when referring to this voice?

…and lastly, how do you feel having just done this exercise?

At this stage it's worth stopping for a moment to take stock. You have gained a deeper awareness of what goes on inside you:

- You've located a critical part of you that speaks with

negativity and fear

- You've noticed that this critical voice causes anxiety and feelings of low self-esteem in your childlike part
- You've realised there's another part to you, that maybe you've saved for those you love, which is a more encouraging, wise and positive voice, which, if listened to, leaves your childlike part feeling more able and less afraid

Now, it's time to look at these parts in more depth to ascertain why they do what they do and see what you can do to take the reigns.

Chapter 4

Some Theory (My own — unexamined in a lab but a theory nonetheless)

One reason the critical voice in your head is often referred to as the Parent is because, for a lot of people, it is an internalised version of one or both of their own critical or fearful parents. But before we lay into our parents for our difficult childhoods let's just stop and think about this for a moment.

Children need that guiding parental voice (both externally and internally) in order to be able to survive physically and in society. The problem starts when we become an adult, but remain plugged into the voice of fear or criticism and believe what it says above everything else.

Of course, some criticism from our parents is natural and right. If one of my daughters wallops her sister you can be sure she gets criticised for it! Similarly, ensuring our children have a healthy respect for danger is good parenting. I am not intending to cast blame on critical parenting or those mums and dads who get scared on behalf of their kids sometimes. It's a given that children need lots of love and encouragement within healthy boundaries and I'm not for a minute belittling the difficult feelings and behaviours that result from a traumatic childhood. What I intend to demonstrate at this stage is that the voice of our parents or main childhood carers (be they good folk or bad) can become internalised and stay with us into adulthood.

Now, as children we often have to push down our natural instincts (e.g. to run into a road without looking, to eat sugar until we pass out, to stay up too late, etc.) and obey the parental voice because we are being prepared for the rigours, freedoms and responsibilities of adulthood. The difficulty arises when our gut instinct (authentic voice or 'wisdom-in-training' if you like) is pushed so far down that we lose it, can't hear it, or treat it like a stranger. When this happens, we enter adulthood with a complete inability to trust ourselves and consequently we rely on that fearful critical voice for guidance and truth. In short, we start our adult lives a bit lost to ourselves.

This point can be further illustrated from my client files. Those who grew up in a dysfunctional home (with severe competition, addiction, neurosis, violence or similar) are, one would assume, the most likely candidates for low self-esteem and a loud, persistent critical voice. And to a degree, this is, of course, true and obvious. However, over half of my clients grew up in what we would describe as normal, loving homes and yet they also have low self-esteem and a loud, internalised critical voice.

The media plays its part in undermining us, as do some teachers, the 'system', our socio-economic status, etc., but, for me, the bottom line is that if we enter adulthood believing that the Critic is telling the truth (rather than listening to our deeper selves), we are going to lack confidence and self-esteem. It's not what happens to us as children, or in our marriages, or at work that causes our fear-based low self-esteem. It's our fearful interpretation today of those things that once happened that causes our pain.

At some point in our development, probably around our late teens, we need to be enabled to find our own wise voice and start listening to it. For many of us this hasn't happened and so we remain locked into the belief that what the Critic in our heads says is always true. But it's not! Accessing and listening to your wiser, deeper, authentic voice will balance out the fear, neutralise the neurosis and ease the anxiety.

With all this in mind, I think it's more helpful and healthy to think of this internalised voice of fear as the Critic rather than the Parent from now on. After all, most parents are doing their best with the tools they've been given, and to blame your folks for all of your 'stuff' is playing the victim, which disempowers you and keeps you stuck. For this reason, I'll be referring to this voice from now on as the Critic but of course you can insert your own name if it helps you. This is the first voice you located — the one that likely lives in or near your head.

Who's Who?

Chapter 5

The Critic (Fear)

When I first identified my critical voice I wanted to do away with it completely. I was so frustrated and saddened that I'd wasted so many years listening to its fearful exaggerations that now I felt I had its number, I was going to rid myself of it and its poison for good!

Thankfully, I had a wise mentor who told me this wasn't possible and enabled me to see that my wishing to get rid of it completely was a form of perfectionism and control. This voice was a part of me and to get rid of it would be akin to cutting off my own arm — an unnecessary act of self-rejection.

What I learned was that each part of me served a purpose and had a motivation, and that if I could uncover those, I would then be able to effectively manage each voice (rather than get rid of those I wasn't so keen on). This seemed like a lengthy process to me (and it wasn't easy) but it was foundational to my future happiness and peace of mind. In short, I'm glad I listened to the wisdom of my forerunners and did as I was told for once!

So, let's get to know your voices more intimately…

The Critic — rooted in FEAR, lives in the head, highly subjective

I deliberately left the following descriptions until after you'd located your own 'voices' to avoid interfering with your process. However, if any of the descriptions below help you better define what's going on in your head then please adopt them as your own. This list is not exhaustive — for every person who does this work we could probably add a new name to the list.

That Voice	The Angry Godhead
The Worrier	The Blamer
The Fortune Teller	The Sphinx
The Dictator	The Saboteur
The Mood Hoover	The Controller
The Mind Reader	The Lower Self
The Gremlin	The Sceptic
The Bully	The Perfectionist
FEAR	The Doubter

The key thing you need to know about the Critic is that it is motivated by **fear**. It is fearful and it uses fear to control you. Fear (both healthy and unhealthy, it isn't choosy) is its currency and its stock in trade. If you feel fear you are likely plugged into what your Critic is saying.

What does your Critic want?

Trainee coaches learn that 'all behaviour has a positive intention' and that if we can source the intention of an action (or thought) we can better understand how to help our clients act in healthier, wiser ways in future. Now, obviously this isn't a live coaching session so I can't elicit the exact motivations of your critical voice, but experience with my clients has taught me that every internalised Critic wants (as a bare minimum) the following:

- To keep you safe
- To be heard

This means that all those times it was telling you not to go for something or that something terrible might happen were because it wanted to protect you and to keep you safe. This is the voice that yells *RUN!* when faced with physical danger. It has a purpose, which is to keep you alive. The problem is, when it comes to our emotional, mental and spiritual growth, it can't always be trusted (even though it means well). Some theories suggest this voice is the more primordial part of us, interested only in survival. Others think it's our more rational, logical, analytical part — our 'left brain' — and if these descriptions help you then please use them.

The point here is to understand that this voice is motivated to keep you safe and to stay in control — in short, to not be in danger. It does not want you to get hurt and it associates emotional pain with physical pain. It has no concept of emotional pain leading to personal growth and, for the Critic, the status quo is where it feels safe so why rock the boat? This voice wants certainty, control and security and will do its utmost to ensure it gets them.

The Critic has learnt from previous negative experiences that failure, rejection and sorrow feel terrible and it associates these feelings with a threat to its survival. Of course, we know as evolved human beings that feelings of failure, rejection and sorrow are an inevitable fact of life and that we can, if we so choose, learn and grow from them.

But the Critic doesn't know this — it operates on fear and security and will always fight to maintain the latter.

This part of your brain struggles to accept the fact that life is uncertain — it wants all its ducks in a line and is therefore engaged in a permanent, futile struggle to get and keep them there. This is why, when you get those odd moments of peace (when the Critic can't find anything to hassle you with) you engage in what I call 'the lighthouse search' for something to worry about. Oh yes, you're not the only one who does this! You search your brain, worried that you've forgotten to worry about something and when you find something new to worry about you're almost relieved to be back on familiar territory.

Crazy but true, yes?

Mad as it might be sometimes, can you see why you can't get rid of this voice? It has a role to play. It's a primitive part of us that serves a purpose. It ensures we (and those we are responsible for) stay safe. You **can** trust it for your physical survival but it is wise to learn to challenge what it says when it comes to the rest of your life.

The second thing the Critic needs — to be heard — is the most interesting to me. I've worked with many, many people who are very aware of the chatter in their heads and tell me their way of dealing with it is to 'just ignore it' (either by pushing the thoughts away, getting drunk, over-eating or using any number of other distraction techniques). But guess what? If it senses it's being ignored this voice just gets louder! That's because it has a job to do — to keep you safe — and it will do this to the death! Referring to our emotional life, the great psychiatrist and psychotherapist Jung said, 'what you resist persists' and he was bang on! The more you resist your thoughts, the more they persist. This may seem counterintuitive but hear me out. There's a huge difference between hearing what someone has to say and doing what they tell you to do. The same applies to your Critic. It can't be ignored but, similarly, it doesn't have to be obeyed.

So, the Critic needs to be acknowledged and heard. If there's an angry, aggressive dog approaching you and your children then listen to the voice of fear and get out of the way. Protect yourself and your children. Similarly, if you're habitually spending more money than you are making then listen to this voice and take action. But if you are plagued by fear and anxiety from the Critic's incessant waffling on about things that might happen in future, what you 'should' or 'shouldn't' be, that you're not good enough, that you might fail, people might think badly of you etc., etc., then thank it for its opinion, tell it that all will be well and seek within yourself for a wiser answer. At this point your Critic is speaking out of turn and needs to be managed (a method for which we will learn later on).

Got it? You decide whether your Critic should be obeyed or not. It is not in charge, **you are**!

How to notice when you are listening to the Critic:

- You feel **fear**: anxious, empty, panicky
- You are off in the future, worrying
- You are stuck mentally in the past, ruminating
- You are blaming someone else for how you feel
- You are trying to control everything around you

Here are some of the beliefs held (or lies told) by the Critic…

1. The Critic believes, 'Worrying affects outcomes.'

The Critic can convince you that you are affecting the outcome of a situation by worrying about it. I know that I used to believe that if I stopped worrying about my first daughter when she was a baby (she's twelve now) that I would somehow be giving permission for something awful to happen to her. I realise now that this was utter madness but I'm not alone. Some people wear their concern like a badge of honour — a way to prove how much they love and care about a person or a situation. But worrying changes nothing — all it does is keep you locked in a negative thought cycle. Worrying is the most fruitless activity on the planet but your Critic speaks this language fluently and frequently.

2. The Critic believes, 'I can't cope.'

This is a lie — a total and utter lie. If one person has coped with something then so can you! You might not like what life throws your way but believing the Critic when it says you can't cope causes you to live in fear of something that hasn't even happened yet. You can cope and you will cope — especially when you've learnt to manage the Critic.

3. The Critic believes, 'It matters what other people think of me.'

We all need approval from others but if that need for approval is keeping you in an unhappy, frustrated situation then the Critic has been in charge. I believe the happiest people are those who are living authentic lives, which means dropping your concern over what other people think and starting to listen to that quiet voice deep within you. Other people will love you for who you are, and if they don't then why would you want them in your life anyway? The Critic will have you put your need for approval above your need to be yourself — not healthy!

4. The Critic believes, 'If you can't do it perfectly, don't try.'

I could write an entire book on perfectionism, and I would describe myself as a 'recovering perfectionist'. The Critic in my head drove me so hard that I wouldn't start a task unless I knew I could get it finished, perfectly, in one hit. It droned on and on and on about what an imperfect mother I was. Perfectionism, i.e. fear of not getting it 'right', was killing me until I learnt to manage the Critic. Now, I aim for progress (based on my best efforts) not perfection and my shoulders have dropped considerably.

5. The Critic believes, 'My past defines me.'

This may sound harsh but your past only defines you if you believe it does. You **can** change! I know you can because the people I work with are changing all the time. If you grew up lonely that doesn't mean you have to accept loneliness today, it just means that your Critic is used to loneliness and sees it as a safe place. You can choose to work through the issues you have around this area and take steps towards a different future. I'm not saying it's easy but your past really doesn't have to define you.

6. The Critic believes, 'Mistakes are bad.'

I tell my children all the time that mistakes are the most normal and natural part of life. Sometimes they are learning opportunities, at other times they're just mistakes made by fallible humans. I need to remember this myself. Mistakes can cause embarrassment, shame and awkwardness, but really, they are just a mark of our humanness. Believing mistakes are bad is the mistake — and one made by the scared Critic.

7. The Critic believes, 'Your emotions will overwhelm you.'

Many people falsely believe that if they start crying they'll never stop, but that's simply not true. Emotions have a limited energy and once expressed they move on rather like hunger that is satisfied with food. The point is to *experience* the feelings rather than push them away. The Critic does not want you to expose your issues (because this isn't 'safe') but I have never seen anyone truthfully face their issues who isn't both more free and more peaceful on the other side.

8. The Critic believes, 'Bad feelings are to be avoided.'

Fear, sorrow, rejection and dejection are a part of life. To resist them is to resist life. The Critic wants to resist these feelings and will tell you to bury them or become victimised by them. *Why me? Isn't it awful? I dread that happening again...* But that's not the healthy answer and sorrow can't be run away from in the same as that angry dog on your street can. Sorrow can be faced and felt and listened to and then moved on from.

I hope by now you have a better understanding of the Critic and how it can negatively affect your life. Critics come in all shapes and sizes and I'd like to share with you the story of one I met a few years ago.

Meet Tom

Tom was in his early twenties when he came on one of my courses. He was a kind and very able young man who was plagued by insecurity, which left him easily distracted and fidgeting nervously. My overriding memory of him that first time I worked with him was of someone desperate to change.

After the course we started working together on a one-to-one basis and it became clear early on that Tom was being terrorised by the critical voice in his head. This voice was, at that time, the most extreme I'd worked with; it was loud, violent and often threatening. Tom was both terrified and ashamed of this voice and had spent huge amounts of energy trying to ignore it or squash it down. But it just became louder and louder. Tom had been to his GP who had diagnosed generalised anxiety and yet Tom was overwhelmed and oppressed by this voice inside him.

Having found the courage to tell me about this voice (which, in itself, was terrifying for Tom) I suggested he try to do some of the work in this book, but he was simply too afraid of the voice to engage with it. I then suggested he allow me to speak to the voice. His initial reaction was to protect me as he thought the voice might hurt me. I assured him that this wouldn't be the case, that I could handle whatever the voice said and that I really couldn't be shocked by anything that came out. I reminded Tom that the voice just wanted to be heard and that we weren't going to be able to move on until we'd 'outed' it.

And so, showing enormous courage, Tom agreed to let me speak to this voice, trusting me that it would help him with his anxiety. I encouraged Tom to relax and asked him to tell me where the voice lived. He pointed to his head after which I asked him to tell me more about it. It was a Sphinx he said, large, imposing, immovable and stern faced. It spoke with a booming voice and loomed over him. I thanked Tom for the introduction and then asked the Sphinx a series of direct questions to which I received some very direct answers. Here's a snapshot of a much, much longer conversation:

> *What do you want, Sphinx?*
> Everything to be OK
> *Why do you shout so loudly at Tom?*
> Because he doesn't listen to me and he gets things wrong all the time.
> *What are you afraid of?*
> Not being listened to.
> *Why are you violent and inappropriate sometimes?*

To get Tom's attention!

What do you need from Tom?

To be heard. I want to be heard...

At this point, Tom opened his eyes and looked at me with what can only be described as joy and relief and said, "It's shrinking, it's shrinking! It's like a tiny little Lego man in my hand right now!"

Tom realised that the voice was a part of him that needed managing and nurturing. That, in fact, it *needed* him and he was in charge (not the voice). His entire demeanour changed as relief and realisation washed over him. He was free. It was one of the most powerful moments I have ever experienced as a coach.

In that moment Tom realised that he had the power. He'd been allowing this fearful voice to run the show for years but actually the voice just wanted a place in Tom's life. Towards the end of the exercise Tom made peace with that part of himself and promised not to ignore it in future. But he also realised that this voice was not a big, scary, stone Sphinx but more like the tiny little Lego man he could hold in the palm of his hand.

Within weeks Tom was happy and confident enough to stop coaching and he continues to maintain his emotional life by practicing this work alone, and has since built a successful career.

Review

Things to remember about this voice:

- It wants to be safe and uses fear to control you
- Its job is to protect you (to survive)
- It wants to be heard
- It lives in the past and/or the future
- It has a back catalogue of past disasters to refer you to and can't see a bright future
- If you ignore it, it will get louder
- If you acknowledge it, it will calm down
- If you feel fearful, anxious or stressed you are likely believing this voice

Get to know your Critic better

- Ask the Critic what it wants…
- Ask it what it's afraid of…
- Ask what it needs in order to feel safe…
- Ask what its core belief is…
- Ask what it would need to be at peace…

A little ritual

The Critic is not your enemy and I really don't want you think it is. This voice has **served** you — it's got you this far and you've survived! So, be grateful to your Critic.

However, it's time for a revolution. If you choose this path, the Critic will be overthrown as the leader of your life. You would probably be wise to give it a job within your top team — it could become Vice President or leader of the opposition, for example.

Remember, you need your Critic sometimes but it's not leader material — it's too prone to panic and despair. You have a wiser, kinder, stronger, more proactive voice within you that was born to lead. So, have a little ritual in which you metaphorically or literally reposition the Critic in your life. Write it a 'Dear John' letter or draw a picture of your new set up. Find a ritual and do it — whatever it takes to tell your subconscious that times are changing, that a new boss is moving in, that there's going to be a cabinet reshuffle. Thank the Critic for its dedicated service thus far and reassure it that, in its new role, it will be heard and useful and safe.

But, just before we get to know your new leader it's time to meet the Child…

A note about fear:

Fear is a part of life and it's an appropriate emotion to feel in some situations. If you or someone you love is under threat it would be appropriate to feel afraid. If you are growing as a person you will likely experience fear — that's normal! But, when your life becomes rooted in and driven by fear you have a problem. It's not healthy to be always afraid. The key to a happy life is balance. You are never going to reach a state of permanent non-fear and you don't have to live in permanent dread. The middle ground is a healthy trust that you can cope with whatever life throws at you and to deal with the thing that's immediately in front of you.

Chapter 6

The Child (Feeling Centre)

The Child
The Rebel
The Victim
The Feeling Centre
The Escape Artist
The Freedom-seeker
The Vulnerable
The Hider
The Reactor

As you can see from the descriptions above, your childlike part can be one or a mixture of many things, however the most important point to remember in this context is that this is your Feeling Centre.

If you are feeling anxious and there is no apparent physical danger then you are likely to be believing a thought from the Critic that is causing that anxiety. Our mission in this work is to find those thoughts and start choosing new ones in order to feel calmer, less anxious and more positive. After all, worrying never solved anything, right?

Some of the people I've worked with have a definite childlike 'voice' inside them that they can access easily. Others literally feel this part of them, identifying it more through their physicality (feeling shaky, blushing, feeling hot, blood rushing through veins, shortness of breath, feeling out of sorts, tension in the neck, jaw, etc.).

When I began this work myself I gave that part of myself a voice in order to access what was really going on inside me. As time has progressed, I no longer do this but I am alerted to negativity or stress by how I feel in my body. You will find your own way with this and there is no 'right or wrong' system — you just need to make the connection to, and listen to, your feelings.

I'll be referring to this second part of you interchangeably as 'the Child' and 'the Feeling Centre' from now on. The analogy of a child works well, as it embodies the sense of powerlessness and reactivity we can experience but the way to identify this is through your feelings. Having said that, please use your own description of this part of you if that works best.

In general terms, your Child could be described as the passive, reactive voice. In essence, it has a feeling reaction to the thoughts you entertain. If the Critic is persistent and loud (as it mostly tends to be) then the Child tends to want to either rebel, hide or escape. This is how it reacts to that voice, especially after having tried very hard to do what it's been told for so long.

Rebellion could involve drinking too much, promiscuity, gossiping about a person, deliberately sabotaging plans, etc. It's when you think, *Enough with all this pressure!* and hit the f**k-it button.

A brilliant example of this from my own past was the constant self-inflicted pressure I put myself under (via the Critic) to be thin. This resulted in strict dieting for a period of time before inevitably (and without fail) finding myself caving in and binge eating (the feeling reaction) before starting the whole darn process again. I did this on and off for over 25 years. Only when I started listening to that wiser, kinder voice (one that suggested I enjoy and accept the lovely body I actually had) did all that dieting and bingeing stop. It wasn't my weight that was the problem; it was my belief system (based on those awful thoughts,) that was wonky.

I believed that being a UK size 12 meant I was 'too big', which caused me to be at war with my body. Today I am blissfully free from all that. Today, I see that there is a range of healthy and normal and it's my job to nurture and enjoy the body I've been given. I eat normally (while avoiding certain trigger foods), I exercise because I love it, I dress for the (frankly, normal) body I have and the relief has been immense.

Hiding is a general term to describe the inertia or stalemate some people find themselves in — either in their work, relationships or their health. Think about it, if you've been listening to a voice that tells you 'you can't' for many years you have probably started to believe it and this has resulted in not a lot of action. I know someone who is amazing at his job — we're talking AMAZING — but he doesn't believe this fact. Instead, he believes the voice of doubt and consequently hasn't progressed in his career and doubts his abilities to do other things as well.

If you want to meet a new partner but spend your Saturday nights unhappily alone with the TV and a takeaway for company, chances are you might be in hiding, having listened to the Critic tell you there's no one out there for you anyway. Hiding can also manifest in denial — when a person detaches themselves from the very real feelings they are experiencing in order to try to avoid the pain they are in.

Escape is often the extreme childlike manifestation of a lifetime of listening to the Critic. It's when you want to run away from your life and responsibilities, quit and/or, in extreme cases, take your own life. It can also be seen when people storm off from an argument or begin over-sleeping or chronic TV watching. Some people escape into addiction and others into their work. Escape, like rebellion and hiding, is a form of avoidance and is a reactive, short-term response to the nagging from the Critic.

Meet Jude

Jude came to me initially for some business coaching. She ran a successful business and had started another, which was struggling. She was also raising a family with her husband and was feeling the pressure of keeping many balls in the air. We established some goals for our work together and made plans for our following session a fortnight later.

The first thing I thought when I saw Jude at her second session was, *What's happened?* She looked haunted. She then told me that she'd left home and was living in a hotel. At this point we established that Jude might be having a breakdown and should see her GP (which she did). We parked the business coaching for a time and instead started exploring the work you find in this book.

In leaving home, Jude was in escape mode. Coaching uncovered a loud Critic in her head manifesting as a controlling perfectionist. Jude had been hooked into this voice for many, many years but had reached breaking point. Her home life was unstable and her second business was shaky, meaning that the perfectionist in her head was panicking loudly until one day her Feeling Centre said, *Enough!* and ran away.

Thankfully Jude didn't stay in the hotel too long and was soon back with her family. Once she'd accepted what was happening to her and had reluctantly started to see that she might be a bit of a perfectionist, she began to get better. She began to make the connection between this perfectionism and her anxiety. She then started to see that there was a gentler, kinder way to approach life, which left her feeling more able to deal with all she had to face.

What does your Child want?

Again, I can't elicit the exact motivations of your Feeling Centre but experience with my clients has taught me that every childlike part of us wants (as a bare minimum) the following:

1. To feel safe
2. To feel free

For the Child, safety is about unconditional love and acceptance more than it is about physical security (which, as we've established, is the remit of the Critic). In very real terms, when a child feels loved and accepted they develop normally and the same applies to your inner life. This part of you also wants to be free to explore, express authenticity and laugh. This part of you, when well cared for, is playful, inspired, carefree and free to love.

The Child in this process

How do you know when you've hurt your body? You feel pain, right? And this pain then causes you to take action to fix the damage.

In the same way, your Feeling Centre can be used to alert you to the damaging thoughts you are allowing yourself to believe. So, if you feel scared, anxious or low then this is likely to be connected to an unhelpful thought from the Critic. (We'll come on to how we can rectify this in a later chapter).

An example

Imagine you're busy at work and your boss rushes in to point out a mistake you made the previous day. Your boss isn't rude but neither is she particularly gentle because she's in a rush and just needs to communicate the error to you before she goes onto another meeting.

How do you react?

Many people will typically react by becoming cross, defensive or weepy. Why? If you react like this I believe it's because what your boss says connects to and echoes what you are saying to yourself. If your Critic says, *You see? I told you this job was too much for you! Well, don't let anyone know that you're struggling because you'll lose your job and then you won't be able to eat or pay the bills...* then you will experience fear and panic in your Feeling Centre, which will cause you to be cross, defensive and/or weepy. You may even try to garner support for your position (because you are scared) by gossiping about your boss with your colleagues and elevating yourself above the situation. All of which is a pretty extreme reaction to the simple fact that as a flawed human being you made a mistake, which your boss pointed out to you because it was her job to do so.

Now, imagine you are plugged into a kinder, wiser voice that tells you it's OK to make mistakes and that everything will work out as it should. You might then be able to separate who you are from the mistake you made and apologise to your boss for the error. You might also ask for a meeting with her as you've been feeling swamped in the role and would like her help to feel more confident with your workload. Suddenly, your Feeling Centre has moved from a reactive place to a proactive place. It's not personal any more but your focus has remained on getting the job done well. Your self-respect and self-esteem are intact.

So, your childlike part can be reactive, hot headed and negative, or, proactive, calm and positive. The latter is where we're headed (probably not all of the time but certainly most of the time).

In short

- When you listen to the Critic you (or your childlike Feeling Centre) feel afraid, anxious and stressed
- When you listen to the Wise Adult inside, you (and your childlike Feeling Centre) feel empowered and more peaceful

So, we're going to learn to start listening more to the Wise Adult buried inside.

Review

Things to remember about the Child/ Feeling Centre:

- Your Feeling Centre is your barometer of how healthy your thoughts are
- Your Feeling Centre needs to be nurtured like a real child

- In response to the Critic it rebels, hides or escapes
- It wants to be safe
- It wants to be free

Get to know your Child better

- Ask the Child what it wants…
- Ask it what it's afraid of…
- Ask what it needs in order to feel safe…
- Ask what its core belief is…
- Ask what it would need to be at peace…

Chapter 7

The Adult (Wisdom)

Wisdom	God
Higher Self	Love
Life	The Negotiator
The Diplomat	The Observer
Truth	Faith
Consciousness	Balance
The Wise Adult	Peace
The Loving Parent	Acceptance

Another caveat

In Chapter 1 I promised you an awkward topic, and here it is. I need to put the 'spirituality' cards out on the table, as they can have an influence on this work. You absolutely do not need to have a spirituality to successfully apply these principles to your life. I used to belong to a religious tradition but these days, I most definitely do not. However, I have retained a spirituality, which helps me greatly in my life. Why? Because, for me it is the embodiment of the wisdom I seek to help me make calmer, more loving and peaceful decisions in my life.

I think that very much like eating and exercising keep our bodies healthy, and cuddling and chatting keep our hearts healthy, the very act of prayer (to whatever you fancy, quite frankly) and meditation has a healthy effect on our mind and our spirits. In fact, neuroscience has proven the calming effects of prayer and meditation on the human brain.

What do I connect to in prayer and meditation? I have no idea, really! I have simply accepted the evidence that stopping and seeking answers from inside (and at the same time) outside of myself works. I am calmer, nicer and wiser as a result. Just as a thrice-weekly trip to the gym ensures my body stays in shape, so daily meditation and prayer keep my mind, heart and soul in shape.

Having said that, if spirituality isn't for you, then your Adult voice will likely be the embodiment of a wise person you know, someone famous you admire, an element of nature, etc. From here you can imagine what they might suggest in any given situation. Or, you can imagine what you would say to your friend if they were facing the same tricky dilemma you find yourself in. It really doesn't matter what imagery you use as long as it helps you connect to a wiser, calmer, kinder part of yourself — imagined or real.

In essence your Adult voice is the voice you use when you're speaking to someone vulnerable. It is the part of you that's able to say, *It's OK, I'm here, everything's going to be alright. Now, what can you do to improve this right now?* So, if you don't want to meditate or pray you can spend time quietly contemplating what your wise friend might say to you about your life.

For this process, the words 'imagine' and 'contemplate' are interchangeable with 'pray' and 'meditate' because all that's important to get going with this work is to find a detached standpoint from which to view your situation.

I often tell my coaching clients that we are going on a journey in my helicopter (I don't have one, sadly, it's metaphorical!) in order to observe their situation from a new angle. The Wise Adult voice inside or outside of you has this objectivity — it is loving, neutral, objective, kind, wise and unafraid. The point of finding this part of you is to hold yourself at a distance for a minute in order to see yourself more clearly.

What does this Wise Adult voice want?

Your Wise Adult voice wants you to grow, to develop, to fly! I believe (although I don't actually and empirically know) that this is the voice great artists listened to as they did their finest work and the most courageous explorers plugged into as they were planning their next expedition. This is the voice that enables a single mother of three to foster a troubled teenager, because she knows that in stretching herself she will grow in love and understanding of herself and others. This is the voice that whispers to you that everything will be OK as long as you continue to love and to learn. This voice is endlessly loving, wise, curious and fun loving. This voice knows how to live and its job is to help you do exactly that to the best of your ability.

I believe that the majority of us have either forgotten we have this voice or have never learned to listen to it. At the very least, if you have any kind of issue with low self-esteem, low confidence, procrastination, anxiety, fear, control, etc. I reckon it's because you don't listen to this voice. You've grown used to the voice of fear and you're now too afraid to ignore it in case it's right. But it's not. The Wise Adult voice within you is right. We've been listening to the critical voice of fear for so long we think it's telling the truth, but is it really? Yes, terrible things can happen to us as people but does worrying about them change anything? No! How about accepting that awful things happen sometimes and listening to the voice that tells you that you will be able to cross that bridge if and when you need to.

Now you are free to focus on making the most of your life

today, unfettered by worrying about something that may never happen. Plugging into wisdom enables you to live in the now.

I used to be the world's biggest worrier and this made me a terrible control freak. I actually believed that I was stopping awful things happening by worrying about them. I wore my worry like a badge of honour. *Look how much I care about X. I'm so worried!* But did my worrying help 'x' or stop 'y' from happening? No, of course not!

I worried so much about ageing that I forgot to enjoy my (fairly) youthful face in my twenties and thirties. I worried so much about my children's safety when we were out that I couldn't enjoy watching them play. I worried about contracting a terrible disease in my old age meaning, again, I didn't enjoy the abundant health I had at the time. What madness!

Do I worry now that I've learned to listen to the wiser part of me? Sometimes, but nothing like I did before, and it lessens all the time. If I'm afraid, I will go inside my thoughts and ask myself why I feel the way I do. It's usually something along the lines of paying for the retirement I'm not even sure I want (I love my work, why would I ever want to retire?) and then I do business with my thoughts. What actions (if any) can I take now to ensure I have some kind of security in my old age? Am I taking them? If the answer is, *Yes, I'm doing what I can* (which is limited with as many mouths to feed as I have), then I choose to believe that my retirement (if I ever have one) will be worked out. I'm doing my best right now and that's all I can do. That's wisdom talking, right there!

Fear says:

You'll be living alone in a cold studio flat with only baked beans to eat and water to drink.

Faith says:

You are doing your best now with the resources you have at your disposal. You give lovingly and freely to others, you are sewing love into your life. Keep doing your best, all is well, all will continue to be well.

I've learned to listen to the Wise Adult voice because:

- Life is easier and much lighter when I do
- I respond much better to encouragement than I do to fear
- I have years of evidence that demonstrates what it says is true and that I'm kinder and much more successful when I listen to this part of myself

Meet Danny

Danny and I did this work to kick off a series of executive coaching sessions.

Danny was only recently in post having taken the plunge into a new career in his early forties. Foremost in his mind was making a success of this new work for his own self-esteem but also in order to continue providing for his wife and young children. Danny was (and still is) incredibly capable at the work and a brilliant team player. However, some negative experiences in his previous company (in a different role) had left him lacking in confidence to deal with stress and confrontation.

So, I asked him to locate his critical voice and to tell me what it said about a particular incident in his previous job. It began to speak about not being able to cope, being bad at confrontation and failure. Danny's body was physically remembering this experience by tensing and reddening in the face. Once the critical voice had been heard, I asked Danny to identify how he was feeling and he said he was feeling dejection, failure and fear.

At this point I asked Danny to imagine someone really wise from that company who might be able to help us see things differently. He immediately described someone he admired greatly and I asked him to imagine what this wise person would speak into the situation had he been there. Danny immediately spoke calming words to himself, giving an objective, balanced point of view and reminding Danny that he had done his best. I then pointed out to

Danny that this wise person was in fact himself, that he'd found the words and spoken them himself.

He was amazed. He hadn't realised it but he had an untapped source of wisdom, confidence and calm within him that he could access at any point in the future. When plugged into this voice he felt far more able to cope with stress and confrontation. He says:

> "Throughout my life I'd always had this critical voice in my head telling me, *You're not good enough,* or, *You'll never make that work.* This voice had become normal for me so naturally I assumed it was always right. I became fearful in every new situation, feeling that anything I did achieve was fraudulent. This made me very frustrated and I became exhausted by this daily internal battle.
>
> This coaching exercise suddenly made me realise that this voice didn't have to control how I felt. Within me was this wise, rational voice that would say things like, *You've been in similar situations before, you've done this before, you can do this again*, or, *It's understandable that you're nervous about this big change, what can you do to break this down into smaller steps?* I also found that imagining this wise voice as somebody I respected helped me to listen carefully to what they were telling me.
>
> The critical voice is still there, it still tells me, *You can't do this!* every so often. However, instead of letting this voice control my feelings, I now listen to what the voice is telling me but then ask my Wise Adult voice, *How do I do this?*
>
> I now find that the critical voice can sometimes be useful to me. It can often be a trigger that some aspect of my life needs looking at. However, I now know that I'm in control of the voices and my feelings. I decide which ones I listen to."

Review

Things to remember about this voice:

- The Adult is the embodiment of wisdom
- The Adult is able to go with the flow and is accepting of life as it is
- The Adult can make decisions with more objectivity than the Critic
- It wants you to grow
- It is fair, balanced and kind

Get to know your Wise Adult better

- Ask the Wise Adult what it wants…
- Ask it what you should do when you're afraid…
- Ask what its core belief is…
- Ask it whether it's up to the job of running the show…
- Ask it what would life would be like if it were in charge of your thoughts…

A note about meditation (or contemplation if you find spirituality off-putting):

Do it! It's the best way to find your inherent wisdom and accessing it on a regular basis means you create a super-highway to peace available to you at anytime of the day or night, wherever you are and whomever you are with. So, find a teacher, download an app such as Headspace, read a book, use a guided meditation thingy on YouTube. I don't mind how you do it, just get mindful. It doesn't have to be in the least bit weird or religious or overly spiritual (unless you want it to be).

I used to think I couldn't meditate because the chatter was so incessant in my head. Meditation has, of course, calmed the chatter down but I also understand now that mindfulness is about allowing the chatter, watching the chatter and noticing the chatter. It's not about clearing out my mind, it's about understanding and accepting what is in my mind. I used to think I didn't have time to meditate — now I think I don't have time not to meditate.

Working It

Chapter 8

Getting to Know You

I clearly remember an intense period of about six weeks when I dared to delve deep into this work myself by actively trying to see what was going on in my head. (I'd been told as a child that this kind of thing was narcissistic 'navel gazing' so I had some shame around even starting this work but I now see that self-awareness is the very antidote to narcissism and neuroses.)

I'd found the different parts of me (the Gremlin, the Angel Fish and the Wise Friend) but I knew I needed to get to know them better if I was going to be free. I was very confused about the different parts of me and sometimes struggled to define who was speaking when, especially when the lines of what they were saying became blurred. So, how did I delve deeper? I took out my pen and journal and I started writing down what the different parts of me were saying. I dedicated 10 to 20 minutes each evening to writing down the thoughts I was having and the feelings I experienced as a result.

My initial frame for the purpose of this time was literally exploration. My job was to be curious and learn what was going on. I was not to judge my thoughts or try to change them (this was nigh on impossible, of course), but my intention was simply to be curious. At this stage I just needed to know what was going on. So, how did I do it? I wrote a script… I tuned into the different parts of me and asked them to speak about the recurring themes of my life at that time, namely my divorce, my parenting and my body (there were more but these three were dominant). Here are some snapshots of those internal conversations.

The parenting script

Critic: You're such a terrible mother! Shouting at those children will only make them resent you and reject you when they're fully-grown. You should be calm and serene all the time. You can't stick at anything — you always say you're going to be perfectly calm and you've blown it by teatime. You are to blame for everything. You should be more like Lisa; she's always calm with her children. And you should spend more time with them — if you didn't work they'd be happier children. You are screwing them up.

Child: I feel so scared when you speak like that. If they reject me I'll die. This is awful, you're right, I want chocolate, I'm sleepy — I can't cope. I might as well just give up.

Critic: You can't give up! That would be quitting and we don't quit! You just have to do better — stop failing.

Child: OK, tomorrow I'll force myself to be perfectly calm. I'm worried I'll screw up again though.

The divorce script

Critic: You've broken the code. Decent people don't leave their marriages. You've screwed up your children and utterly ruined their lives. You've betrayed your partner. You are not who I thought you were. People will hate you and they have every right to. You should've pushed your feelings down and stayed in your marriage. Your happiness is not as important as his. You will never be forgiven for this.

Child: I feel sick. I will always feel terribly about this. I had to leave — I wish I was a more committed person.

The body script

Critic: You will only be acceptable if you're a size 8–10 and weigh under 140lbs. You need to lose weight. Being a size 12–14 is too big. You are too big. Your stretch marks are disgusting — who's going to want a woman with wobbly skin on her stomach? You must eat less. You must stop eating all carbs and sugar. You must be thin, it's the only way you're going to be happy.

Child: You're right — my body is ugly. I will start another diet tomorrow so now I'm going to eat everything I can and then I will never eat sweet, fatty or carby stuff again.

Can you see the patterns? The Critic (which I believed to be the voice of absolute truth) gave me a pretty hard time using criticism, perfectionism and fear to control me. This caused me to **feel** anxious, scared, useless, despondent, etc., and then **react** by either wanting to hide (sleep), escape (I can't cope) or rebel (I'm going to stuff my face with food).

If ever you needed an illustration of a vicious cycle, this is it. Round and round I went with these thoughts, feelings and reactions. It was a negative downward spiral. I kept trying to change the Child but actually I needed to change or challenge the Critic.

When I'd spent some time doing this work with just the Critic and the Child, I then started to introduce the Wise Adult into the mix to see what it might say. I went back over the same scripts (they were pretty repetitive anyway) and added this new voice.

The parenting script (again)

Critic: You're such a terrible mother! Shouting at those children will only make them resent you and reject you when they're fully-grown. You should be calm and serene all the time. You can't stick at anything — you always say you're going to be perfectly calm and you've blown it by teatime. You are to blame for everything.

You should be more like Lisa; she's always calm with her children. And you should spend more time with them — if you didn't work they'd be happier children. You are screwing them up.

Child: I feel so scared when you speak like that. If they reject me I'll die. This is awful, you're right, I want chocolate, I'm sleepy — I can't cope. I might as well just give up.

Critic: You can't give up! That would be quitting and we don't quit! You just have to do better — stop failing.

Child: OK, tomorrow I'll force myself to be perfectly calm. I'm worried I'll screw up again though.

Wisdom: Let's look at this calmly for a minute. The children were behaving pretty badly so it would take a saint to remain perfectly calm all the time. Give them a cuddle, tell them you love them and forgive yourself. Sometimes you will shout — that's life. Perfection is a myth, remember?

Child: That's true — I can't be perfect but I can give them a hug. They are lovely…

And this was when I had my breakthrough moment. I realised that when I listened to the angry, scared, bossy, critical voice I felt anguished, fearful and panicky all the time. However, now when I accessed and listened to my Wise Adult voice I felt calmer, more empowered, more able. My Critic had prevented me from owning my part in various disagreements I had (because it demanded perfection and control) but the wiser voice enabled me to be human and flawed therefore meaning I could give the kids a hug and move on rather than trying to hide or deny what was going on. In short, accessing wisdom released truth and we all know that the truth sets us free, right? This was fascinating to me. I tried it again.

Back to the body script

Critic: You will only be acceptable if you're a size 8–10 and weigh under 140lbs. You need to lose weight. Being a size 12–14 is too big. You are too big. Your stretch marks are disgusting — who's going to want a woman with wobbly skin on her stomach? You must eat less. You must stop eating all carbs and sugar. You must be thin, it's the only way you're going to be happy.

Child: You're right — my body is ugly. I will start another diet tomorrow so now I'm going to eat everything I can and then I will never eat sweet, fatty or carby stuff again.

Wisdom: You don't have to stuff yourself with food today if you can decide not to diet tomorrow. Severe restrictive dieting is where the problem starts. Trying to change your body is the problem, not your weight. Rather than trying to change your body, try accepting it as it is today and see how you feel and how you eat. Acceptance is the beginning of change.

Child: That's a bit radical! I've been trying to get smaller all my life! But I am so fed up with dieting — it's like being in jail.

Wisdom: You don't have to panic about your weight right now. Try something new — try eating healthy foods when you're hungry and see what happens.

Child: I know I'm just falling for media brainwashing and I do have a nice shape. I'm just scared to let go of this. I'm scared I'll get fat.

Wisdom: No-one who eats normally gets fat. Just try a day without trying to change your body. Just see what it feels like to 'be' in the body you have and eat for nourishment and health.

After this piece of writing I gained a glimmer of hope that maybe I could be OK with my body someday. That at least a part of me liked my body. This was breaking news as far as I was concerned and the results have been incredible.

I then tried introducing wisdom into my most painful script, my divorce.

The divorce script (again)

Critic: You've broken the code. Decent people don't leave their marriages. You've screwed up your children and utterly ruined their lives. You've betrayed your partner. You are not who I thought you were. People will hate you and they have every right to. You should've pushed your feelings down and stayed in your marriage. Your happiness is not as important as his. You will never be forgiven for this.

Child: I feel sick. I will always feel terribly about this. I had to leave — I wish I was a more committed person.

Wisdom: It takes two people to cause the downfall of a relationship and you were both unhappy. Casting blame isn't going to fix this. It's OK to want to be happy. Focus on doing your best for the kids. This will work out in time.

Child: You're right. I still hate the fact that I've broken something even though I didn't feel I had any other choice.

Wisdom: Then maybe you can accept that this is not what you would've chosen but it is your reality?

Child: Yes, I can accept that.

What I've shown you above is a mere snapshot of the dialogues and scripts I wrote all that time ago. You don't need to see the ins and outs. The point of showing you is to illustrate just how loud and (frankly) abusive my critical voice was and how scared it made me. When I accessed the Wise Adult voice, I calmed down. It was pretty simple.

From here I assumed that I could just listen to the Adult all the time and get rid of the Critic but, as I said earlier in the book, this isn't possible or healthy. What I learnt was that the Adult voice was sometimes called upon to mediate between the Critic and the Child especially when the Critic was in full throttle. So my scripts developed even further. Let's look at the divorce script again.

Back to the divorce script

Critic: You've broken the code. Decent people don't leave their marriages. You've screwed up your children and utterly ruined their lives. You've betrayed your partner. You are not who I thought you were. People will hate you and they have every right to. You should've pushed your feelings down and stayed in your marriage. Your happiness is not as important as his. You will never be forgiven for this.

Child: I feel sick. I will always feel terribly about this. I had to leave — I wish I was a more committed person.

Wisdom: It takes two people to cause the downfall of a relationship and you were both unhappy. Casting blame isn't going to fix this. It's OK to want to be happy. Focus on doing your best for the kids. This will work out in time.

Child: You're right. I still hate the fact that I've broken something even though I didn't feel I had any other choice.

Wisdom: Then maybe you can accept that this is not what you would've chosen but it is your reality?

Child: Yes, I can accept that.

Wisdom: Critic, why do you say these things about the divorce?

Critic: Because I'm afraid if I don't then someone else will. It's easier to hear it from myself than from someone else. At least if I'm saying it the opinions of other people won't be a shock and I'll be prepared.

Wisdom: So you're trying to soften the blow from others by being mean to yourself. You're trying to second guess the future — control it?

Critic: Yes, I guess. I feel it really was wrong, though — to end the marriage was wrong.

Wisdom: Even if you were unhappy?

Critic: I should've tried harder.

Wisdom: But maybe you'd been trying for years and years and had run out of steam.

Critic: That's true.

Wisdom: What do you need?

Critic: I need to know that I won't ever end up in this much pain and turmoil again. That I won't cause pain like that to someone else again.

Wisdom: No one wants to go through this but you've survived and grown and the children are doing really well. No one knows what the future holds but having survived this you know you could again if you had to.

Critic: I guess. But I don't want to.

Wisdom: I know. No one does.

And this is what I learnt. The job of the Wise Adult is to speak words of wisdom and truth to both the Critic and the Child. It's the ultimate diplomat and coach as well as your greatest teacher and encourager. This voice will never let you down so you can believe what it says. It takes the needs of both the Critic and the Child into consideration (as well as those of other people in the situation) and gives a fair assessment of the best way forwards.

Over to you...

Success leaves clues and so if you want the emotional and mental freedom I describe in this book then you need to do the work I've done. So, start writing out your own scripts using the templates I link to at the end of this chapter. Write down what's going on inside you.

Dedicate time to this and you will start getting better because you will give your Critic the space it needs to be heard and you will access and empower the Wise Adult to speak more freely. Once you are used to accessing and listening to this voice, believing it will become easier and easier. Remember, reluctance is part of this. You probably won't want to do this but you absolutely won't regret it if you do. You are worth this investment of time and the initial pain of getting started. It's just 10–20 minutes each day — so go on, give it a try.

If you can spend time every day (or most days) for four–six weeks writing down the script that rolls around in your mind you will achieve several things:

- Much greater self-awareness, i.e. you'll know yourself better, which is a good thing
- You will gave the knowledge that you do have a choice over the thoughts you believe

- You will have the freedom to make this choice on a minute-by-minute basis, which is outlined in the next chapter

*You'll find scripting worksheets at the back of this book and can download more, free from my website: jo-emerson.com/flying-for-beginners.

Chapter 9

Noticing, Catching and Unhooking

By this stage you will have identified the different parts to your personality and started to see the games played in your mind. You have spent time learning more about yourself and hopefully had some written conversations with yourself.

If you're like the rest of us your Critic will still be waffling on — it doesn't really seem to learn, primordial little beast that it is. But, what you might have realised by now is that you can take what it says or leave it. You can remain plugged into what it says or you can unhook by asking yourself for a wiser, calmer alternative view of the situation in which you find yourself.

From here, having gained access to all of this, you can now start to notice and unhook on a more regular basis. What do I mean by this? I mean that you notice that you are feeling afraid and stop for a second to ask yourself why…? What thoughts are you believing that are causing this fearful state? Now, ask yourself what the voice of wisdom, love and faith might have to offer in this situation and try on that belief for size. Now, how do you feel? Better? Great! Now, choose which version to believe before continuing with your day.

The more you practise this, the better and quicker you will become at it. You will find yourself in the queue at the supermarket feeling angry or worried and will ask yourself what thought you just believed that resulted in this feeling. You will then tap on the door of Wisdom and ask its opinion. Then, seeing the choice of thoughts in front of you, you'll make a decision to either continue to be angry and afraid, or to become accepting and calm. And, if you choose the latter you'll notice a new feeling in your body.

This all sounds rather clunky but it's become second nature to me now to notice a feeling, ask myself what I'm believing and, while I'm there, my mind already starts a conversation with Wisdom, seeking a more helpful version of events.

Let's look at this in action.

Scenario one

Sam notices he feels worried, sick and afraid.

Sam asks himself, *What thought have I been believing?*

Critic: That report you wrote today isn't good enough. You're going to be in big trouble tomorrow.

Sam asks his wiser self to appraise the situation.

Wisdom: The bulk of the report is great and you've worked really hard. It's just the final section that needs more work. Why not email it over to your boss tonight to ask for his help to see what can be added before the meeting tomorrow?

Sam notices he feels less anxious because he has a solution.

Scenario two

Ruby notices she's feeling lonely and fed up. She's been contemplating calling her ex — a relationship she knows isn't good for her…

Ruby asks herself, *What thoughts have I been believing?*

Critic: You're never going to find a decent partner. You're lonely and you'll always be lonely. Everyone else is happily in love and you're facing the rest of your life alone.

Ruby asks her wiser self to appraise the situation.

Wisdom: Being alone is uncomfortable because you haven't done it for a long time but it's better than being in the wrong relationship. This time alone is good for you — it's healing time from the past and preparation time for a good relationship in future.

Ruby notices the panic about her current situation leaving her. She notices panic being replaced with some acceptance.

Of course, there are times when you will continue to feel afraid, angry, resentful or self-pitying and this is normal. However, the better you become at this, the more you will notice that choosing to believe negativity and fear leaves you feeling bad and powerless but that the more you choose to listen to Wisdom the freer you will become. The point is you have accessed the choice over what you feel. And choice over anything is our greatest freedom and privilege as humans.

So remember:

- **Notice** what you are feeling
- **Catch** the negative/fearful thought and ask for a wiser/more loving thought
- **Unhook** from the negative thought and replace it with the wiser sentiment
- Go about your day…

Or, an even quicker way to do this goes something like this…

Ask yourself: Is this thought rooted in fear or wisdom? You know what to do from there.

Chapter 10

Other People's Voices

By this stage you will have learnt a whole heap of new stuff about yourself and how you react to your world. You will have gained a choice over what you believe, which will have given you a choice over the words you speak and the actions you take. You will be gaining a new sense of confidence in your abilities to handle life and whatever it throws your way and you'll have a better command over fear.

This naturally gives you a curiosity about, and a better understanding of, the people you encounter in your day-to-day life. For example, when you come across someone else's anger you can choose to ask yourself which voice of theirs they might be plugged into in that moment. This is not to judge that person but to give you some compassion for where they might be coming from.

We've all encountered an angry driver using expressive hand gestures to communicate his or her rage at our driving ability (or lack of). And, we've all probably reacted with similar use of our fingers, mouths, horns, etc. But, what if you stopped and asked yourself:

Which voice is that driver plugged into? The Critic? They're certainly acting like an angry child (and anger is the fruit of fear). So, maybe a better response would be to ignore them, or wave an apology or let it go because it's not about you, it's about them and whatever other stuff is going on in their life.

Now, you've had an adult, calm response to the situation and can move on with your day. You may even be able to wish that driver well (internally) recognising that you, too, know what it is to be so overwhelmed with negative fear that it once caused you to react to people in ways that maybe weren't so helpful.

Of course, if someone is so angry they are threatening you then you must do whatever you can to protect yourself. My point here is that we so often take other people's anger personally when in fact they are just listening to the negative drivel in their heads because they don't know differently. But you do! So have compassion for them and compassion for yourself. After all, we're all doing our best with the tools we've been given.

Workbook

A space for your notes

The Critic

(Fear)

That Voice
The Worrier
The Fortune Teller
The Dictator
The Mood Hoover
The Mind Reader
The Gremlin
The Bully
FEAR
The Angry Godhead
The Blamer
The Sphinx
The Saboteur
The Controller
The Lower Self
The Sceptic
The Perfectionist
The Doubter

My Critical Voice

Name this voice:

____

Where does this voice live?

____

What does this voice remind you of?

____

What sorts of things does this voice say?

____

____

How do you feel when this voice speaks?

____

____

The Child

(Feeling Centre)

The Child
The Rebel
The Victim
The Feeling Centre
The Escape Artist
The Freedom-seeker
The Vulnerable
The Hider
The Reactor

My Child-like Voice

Name this voice:

___

Where does this voice live?

___

What does this voice remind you of?

___

What sorts of things does this voice say?

___

___

How do you feel when this voice speaks?

___

___

The Adult

(Wisdom)

Wisdom
Higher Self
Life
The Diplomat
Truth
Consciousness
The Wise Adult
The Loving Parent

God
Love
The Negotiator
The Observer
Faith
Balance
Peace
Acceptance

My Adult Voice

Name this voice:

____

Where does this voice live?

____

What does this voice remind you of?

____

What sorts of things does this voice say?

____

____

How do you feel when this voice speaks?

____

____

Scripting sheets

Critic: ____

____

____

Child: ____

____

____

Critic: ____

____

____

Child: ____

____

____

Critic: ____

____

____

Child: ____

____

____

Adult: ____

____

____

____

____

Critic: ____

____

____

Child: ____

____

____

Critic: ____

____

____

Child: ____

____

____

Critic: ____

____

____

Child: ____

____

____

Adult: ____

____

____

____

____

Critic: ______________________________

____

____

Child: ______________________________

____

____

Critic: ______________________________

____

____

Child: ______________________________

____

____

Critic: ______________________________

____

____

Child: ______________________________

____

____

Adult: ______________________________

____

____

____

____

Critic: ____

____

____

Child: ____

____

____

Critic: ____

____

____

Child: ____

____

____

Critic: ____

____

____

Child: ____

____

____

Adult: ____

____

____

____

____

Critic: ______________________________

____

____

Child: ______________________________

____

____

Critic: ______________________________

____

____

Child: ______________________________

____

____

Critic: ______________________________

____

____

Child: ______________________________

____

____

Adult: ______________________________

____

____

____

____

Critic: ____

____

____

Child: ____

____

____

Critic: ____

____

____

Child: ____

____

____

Critic: ____

____

____

Child: ____

____

____

Adult: ____

____

____

____

____

Critic: ____

____

____

Child: ____

____

____

Critic: ____

____

____

Child: ____

____

____

Critic: ____

____

____

Child: ____

____

____

Adult: ____

____

____

____

____

Critic: ____

____

____

Child: ____

____

____

Critic: ____

____

____

Child: ____

____

____

Critic: ____

____

____

Child: ____

____

____

Adult: ____

____

____

____

____

Critic: ____

____

____

Child: ____

____

____

Critic: ____

____

____

Child: ____

____

____

Critic: ____

____

____

Child: ____

____

____

Adult: ____

____

____

____

____

Critic: ____

____

____

Child: ____

____

____

Critic: ____

____

____

Child: ____

____

____

Critic: ____

____

____

Child: ____

____

____

Adult: ____

____

____

____

____

Critic: ____

____

____

Child: ____

____

____

Critic: ____

____

____

Child: ____

____

____

Critic: ____

____

____

Child: ____

____

____

Adult: ____

____

____

____

____

Critic: ____
____
____

Child: ____
____
____

Critic: ____
____
____

Child: ____
____
____

Critic: ____
____
____

Child: ____
____
____

Adult: ____
____
____
____
____

Critic:

Child:

Critic:

Child:

Critic:

Child:

Adult:

Critic: ____

____

____

Child: ____

____

____

Critic: ____

____

____

Child: ____

____

____

Critic: ____

____

____

Child: ____

____

____

Adult: ____

____

____

____

____

Critic: ____

____

____

Child: ____

____

____

Critic: ____

____

____

Child: ____

____

____

Critic: ____

____

____

Child: ____

____

____

Adult: ____

____

____

____

____

Critic: ____

____

____

Child: ____

____

____

Critic: ____

____

____

Child: ____

____

____

Critic: ____

____

____

Child: ____

____

____

Adult: ____

____

____

____

____

Critic: ______________________________

____

____

Child: ______________________________

____

____

Critic: ______________________________

____

____

Child: ______________________________

____

____

Critic: ______________________________

____

____

Child: ______________________________

____

____

Adult: ______________________________

____

____

____

____

Critic: ______________________________
____
____

Child: ______________________________
____
____

Critic: ______________________________
____
____

Child: ______________________________
____
____

Critic: ______________________________
____
____

Child: ______________________________
____
____

Adult: ______________________________
____
____
____
____

Critic: ____

____

____

Child: ____

____

____

Critic: ____

____

____

Child: ____

____

____

Critic: ____

____

____

Child: ____

____

____

Adult: ____

____

____

____

____

Critic: ____

____

____

Child: ____

____

____

Critic: ____

____

____

Child: ____

____

____

Critic: ____

____

____

Child: ____

____

____

Adult: ____

____

____

____

____

Epilogue

This book will give you wings to fly above your thoughts, your life and your interactions with others to see what's really going on. If you're like me, you'll never look back because once you've tasted freedom you'll want to hang on to it. No one can ever clip these wings you've grown through finding your own inner wisdom. Your wisest self has always been there and will always be there. Happy flying!

Further Reading

Games People Play, Eric Berne

Inner Bonding, Margaret Paul

The Undiscovered Self, Carl Jung

The Plastic Mind, Sharon Begley

The Ego and the Id, Sigmund Freud

I would also highly recommend you try the awesome Headspace app available from www.headspace.com, in order to give mindfulness a try. It's totally non-religious, free for beginners and very reasonably priced thereafter.

About the Author

Jo Emerson is a leading confidence coach and human behaviour expert. She works with clients across the globe, helping them to make positive life changes and to achieve their goals for success.

Jo speaks frequently at conferences and events across the UK and has been featured in and written for numerous publications including *The Guardian*, *Good Housekeeping*, *Cosmopolitan*, *Metro*, *US News* and *Prima*.

Sign up to receive Jo's enewsletter on her website, jo-emerson.com where she blogs frequently about how to live a successful, authentic, confident life. There, you will also find information about upcoming events and publications, as well as her new ecourse, *5 Steps to Lasting Confidence*.

You can follow Jo on Twitter and Facebook for regular doses of wisdom, truth and tips for personal development.

Printed in Great Britain
by Amazon

36264860R00078